WIRE TAPPED
AMERICA

WIRE TAPPED AMERICA

CIA Informant Exposes
How "They" Are Watching You
And How You Can Stop It

BY FRANK MITCHELL

FAMILY SURVIVAL
ALWAYS SAFE, ALWAYS PREPARED

Copyright © 2016 by Frank Mitchell, FamilySurvival.com & 5280 Publishing, LLC

All rights reserved. This book or any portion thereof may not be reproduced or used in any manner whatsoever without the express written permission of the publisher except for the use of brief quotations in a book review.

Printed in the United States of America

First Printing, 2016

ISBN 978-0-9974376-5-2

5280 Publishing, LLC dba FamilySurvival.com
453 E. Wonderview Ave.
Estes Park, CO 80517
www.FamilySurvival.com

DISCLAIMER OF LIABILITY AND WARRANTY

This publication describes the author's opinions regarding the subject matter herein. The author and publisher are not rendering advice or services pertaining to specific individuals or situations. For specific advice, or if expert assistance is required, the services of a qualified professional should be obtained. The author and publisher assume no responsibility whatsoever for the use of the information in this publication or for decisions made or actions taken based, in whole or in part, on the information in this publication. The author and publisher make no warranties, express or implied, regarding the information. Without limiting the foregoing, the author and publisher specifically disclaim and will not be responsible for any liability, loss, or risk incurred directly, indirectly or incidentally as a consequence of the use or misuse of any advice or information presented herein. Use this publication and information with good judgment and do the best you can in your particular situation.

You agree to indemnify and hold the author and publisher, and their respective officers, directors, agents, employees, contractors and suppliers, harmless from any claim or demand, including reasonable attorneys' fees, related to your use or misuse of this publication or the information contained therein. You further agree that you will cooperate fully in the defense of any such claims.

Notice: As the purchaser of this publication you are permitted to store it and print it for your own personal use only. Otherwise, no part of this publication may be reproduced, stored in a retrieval system or transmitted in any form or by any means, electronic, mechanical, photocopying, recording, or otherwise without the prior written permission of the copyright owner and publisher. It is illegal to make a copy of all or part of this publication for someone else, even if you do not charge for the copy. If you have purchased this book from anywhere other than FamilySurvival.com, including eBay, please report it to support@familysurvival.support immediately.

COPYRIGHT

Those who have received or purchased the guide are neither authorized nor permitted to transmit copies of this guide to anyone without written permission. Giving away copies to people who haven't paid for them is illegal under international copyright laws and will submit you to possible legal action. Therefore, the utilization of this material is limited to personal use only.

TERMS AND DISCLAIMER

By using, viewing, and interacting with this guide or the FamilySurvival.com website, you agree to all terms of engagement, thus assuming complete responsibility for your own actions.

The authors and publishers will not be held liable or claim accountability for any loss or injuries. Use, view, and interact with these resources at your own risk. All publications from FamilySurvival.com and its related companies are strictly for informational purposes only.

While all attempts have been made to verify the accuracy of information provided on our website and within our publications, neither the authors nor the publishers are responsible for assuming liability for possible inaccuracies. The authors and publishers disclaim any responsibility for the inaccuracy of the content, including but not limited to errors or omissions. Loss of property, injury to self or others, and even death could occur as a direct or indirect consequence of the use and application of any content found herein.

The Central Intelligence Agency is an important part of the intelligence apparatus of the United States. Many of us can't help but feel a little pride for the CIA, the group that is both revered and feared among the intelligence community of the world as the best of the best. Technically speaking, the CIA is a service that is devoted to foreign intelligence and foreign actions. For anything domestic, usually, the Federal Bureau of Investigation (FBI) is the agency of choice. However, that is really just the official party line. The CIA is vehement in official communication that it exists to gather intelligence and perform operations outside the United States, however, there is no way for *you*, the average American, to really know the extent of what they are up to.

Whatever your thoughts are about Wikileaks – the global organization devoted to the gathering and publishing of classified information stolen from world governments, they have recently dealt the CIA a serious blow by releasing a huge cache of classified information about the way CIA hackers are able to penetrate and monitor computers, cell phones, televisions, and even vehicles. Here at Family Survival, we don't want to enter the politics about the correctness or justness of what Wikileaks did; we could sell it to you both ways. In one sense, Wikileaks, or more specifically, the operatives who obtained this classified information are treasonous and not acting in the best interests of America. On the other hand, Americans have the right to know what their government might potentially be doing to them – monitoring, surveilling, influencing, or meddling. We'll leave it at that.

Being practically minded, we now see that we have an opportunity placed before us, an opportunity to study the leaked information so that we can better protect our own privacy. It's a shame that as Americans we need to protect ourselves from our own government, but unfortunately, that's what needs to be done in this day and age. But before we delve in to the impressive hacking capabilities of the CIA, let's makes some critical assumptions:

- We have to assume that the tools used by the CIA are shared with other government intelligence agencies, or at least known by them. The other agencies we are referring to are the NSA and FBI specifically, although there are a dozen or more smaller intelligence agencies in the USA, devoted to gathering intelligence both foreign and domestic.

- We have to assume that the hacking tools discovered by Wikileaks have been deployed against Americans. No matter what the official line is on the CIA website, it must be all but certain that many of these powerful hacks have been used on the American people, if not by the CIA themselves, then by some authorized affiliate.

- We have to assume that the trove of information released by Wikileaks is *far* from complete, meaning the true capabilities of the CIA are much greater than would be revealed by a cache of documents. Think about it for a minute; the CIA has virtually unlimited funding, huge manpower, and the most cutting edge technology on the planet. Of course they can do more than what Wikileaks is telling us...just use your imagination.

THAT SAID, LET'S SEE WHAT THE CIA CAN DO!

Before we delve into super-secret recently leaked CIA hacks, let's keep in mind that what Wikileaks stole was information related to a *CIA hacker group*. Therefore, the CIA's other capabilities – namely espionage, foreign operations, covert assassinations, and other skills were not part of this document trove. This series of leaks deals only with the CIA's computer hacking capabilities – but before you stop reading, keep in mind that computers control everything today. They control your appliances, your power grid, your gas lines, your cell phones, your vehicle's onboard systems, and yes, your computers (obviously). So a CIA hacker is well capable of making your life into complete misery, or even *killing you*, with the flick of a keypad. Computer geeks aren't what they used to be, apparently.

CIA Malware

Don't feel bad if you haven't heard of the term *malware*, which is short for Malicious Software. You probably know all about viruses if you own a computer; viruses have been around since basically the advent of the computer. Viruses are usually destructive or disruptive in nature, their primary purpose being to annoy the user, destroy data, or render the computer inoperable. Malware, on the other hand, is designed not to be detected at all, while covertly performing whatever function the programmer wants – surveillance, data theft, eavesdropping, and many more functions. Malware is created by highly skilled computer programmers sometimes known as hackers, and it takes extreme amounts of skill for the programmer to create software that is stealthy enough to fool another hacker while at the same time performing a covert function. As the Wikileaks trove revealed, the CIA has an entire department full of hackers whose job it is to create malware, and it is this malware that is the driving force behind the CIA's ability to reach out and touch someone.

Again, before you dismiss malware as a nuisance or something that doesn't apply to you, keep in mind that every electronic device you own, every utility that powers and heats your home, and every computer in your car is susceptible to malware. Malware isn't just something you pick up while surfing the internet. Malware can be something placed remotely into your car that prevents your antilock brakes from working....killing you or someone else.

The thrust of what Wikileaks discovered is that the CIA uses malware as a building block for all kinds of evil little technologies that can affect us, no matter how remote or "off grid" we claim to be. We don't think anyone was truly surprised that the CIA or more correctly the US government had such technology, although we are a little surprised in the way this technology is being used.

The Walls Have Ears

One of the leaks in the Wikileaks trove dealt with surveillance by way of smart TV. Smart TVs aren't a particular brand or phenomenon; basically every TV sold in stores today and for the past several years is a smart TV. You probably have one or more of these televisions in your home; they are TVs that can connect to the internet and have built in applications whereby you can watch Netflix or Amazon movies with a push of a button. Many of these TVs can send emails and access the internet through a browser like a computer. Many of them also have remote on and off features that can be controlled when you are away from home, remotely.

The CIA documents reveal that they successfully hacked into Samsung televisions and used them as *surveillance devices* within people's homes. The way they did it was brilliant – with malware. Unbeknownst to the user, the CIA would:

- Covertly infect the TV with malware
- Hijack the on/off switch, such that when the user pressed the off switch, the TV entered what is referred to as "fake off mode"
- *Fake off* mode is devilishly clever. It shuts off the LED lights on the front of the TV, and shuts off the screen, while the rest of the TV – it's brain – *remains on*.

- Then, while in fake off mode, the TV records and transmits what it hears, and sends it back to the CIA. It can even take pictures....all the while the user thinks the TV is off.

Fake off is an engineering masterpiece; that beautiful television you bought and paid for with your hard earned money is hijacked by the CIA, and turned into a listening device that is on 24 hours per day, seven days per week, sending crystal clear HD audio back to Langley, Virginia where the CIA logs every vowel and syllable you utter and stores is *forever*. All those things you said about the president, all those things you idly said to your wife or kids. Every embarrassing, personal moment in your inner sanctum – your living room or bedroom – logged remotely, without you knowing. And, if your TV is capable of it, it took pictures and videos of you too. *Now how do you feel about malware?*

The CIA Can Own Your Phone

Most Americans would generally agree that cell phone conversations aren't really private. Between the news and episodes of *Cops*, we are well aware that phones can be wiretapped and that the police and other federal agencies have long had the ability to listen into our phone calls. But what the CIA can do with your cell phone is an order of magnitude nastier than simply listening in to you your calls, which is child's play.

Using their hackers, the CIA has engineered malware that can infect both Android and iOS (Apple) phones. Before we go further, it should be noted that currently, Android has a market share of 85% globally, while the iPhone only holds a 15% market share. Still, the CIA has invested a disproportionate amount of energy mastering iPhone hacks, because it was noted by them that more public figures, celebrities, government officials and notables used an iPhone than any other type of phone. Basically, the rich and powerful out there are iPhone users, and for whatever reason, these are the people the CIA is most interested in (still think they aren't spying on Americans??)

CIA cellular phone malware is engineered to:

- Forward your texts to the CIA without your knowledge.
- Geolocate you using the phone's GPS to track your movements without your knowledge.

- Use your cell phone as a listening device for your *non telephonic conversations*.
- Forward your pictures to the CIA
- Take pictures and video using your phone's camera without your knowledge.
- Intercept and forward your emails to the CIA.

Unlike police, who have to obtain a search warrant from a judge in order to tap your cell phone or view your phone records, the CIA needs no such approval, and it is capable of doing much more than just listening in to your phone conversations. Much like the way it can control televisions, the CIA can turn the phone that you carry all day and leave beside you at night into the ultimate covert bug.

Do you think you're safe because your cell phone runs an app with encryption (WhatsApp, Signal, Telegram, Wiebo, Confide or Cloackman)? Guess what – CIA malware is designed such that it intercepts the text communication *prior* to encryption. To understand how this works, you need to understand how encryption works in the first place. Normally, you compose a message. When you hit send, the app then encrypts that message, meaning it makes it unreadable to anyone else who does not have the encryption key. The user you sent the message to then receives the encrypted message, and his phone then decrypts the message so it can be read in plain text.

The CIA knows full well that modern encryption algorithms are almost impossible to hack; they would take a room full of daisy chained mainframe supercomputers years to decrypt – that's how powerful encryption is. That's why the CIA doesn't even try to read your encrypted communications. In fact, their malware focuses on reading your plain text messages before they have been encrypted, in that split second it takes from when you hit send to when the message is actually encrypted. Pretty impressive!

Lastly, the CIA goes to great lengths to keep these hacks away from Google and Apple, the makers of Android and iOS respectively. This is because they want to continue exploiting what are essentially gaping holes and design flaws in Google and Apple's programming. This is another reason why the Wikileaks leak is so damaging to CIA efforts; when the manufacturers are alerted of a security hole, they can fix it, which means the CIA needs to find another workaround in order to hack cell phones. Which they most certainly will....

Christine?

Author Stephen King envisioned a car that enjoyed killing its occupants as well as innocent bystanders, but even King could not have foreseen what the CIA is capable of doing with a strategic implantation of malware, and new vehicle construction only helps them further their goal of total vehicle control. For the past decade, vehicles have been increasingly network capable, and most every vehicle built within the past 10 years is capable of being connected to the internet – which of course means that it can be affected by CIA implanted malware.

For vehicles made within the past three years, the following computer features are either standard equipment or offered as an option on most cars for sale in America today:

- Throttle by wire – no cable control of the throttle pedal.
- Steer by wire – no physical steering shaft, just computers controlling motors
- Wi-Fi – in vehicle internet capability.
- Front and rear cameras
- Autonomous and semi autonomous driving capability – meaning advanced cruise controls that can basically steer themselves.

Basically, a modern car is almost completely computer controlled. To show you what that means exactly, we will create a fictional scenario of what could happen with CIA malware:

- You're driving your car on a busy freeway.
- Using the network name of your vehicle and its GPS coordinates, a CIA hacker takes control of your car remotely.
- The hacker floors the gas on your car, which is throttle by wire, and at the same time disables the brake pedal.
- Using your vehicle's GPS, the hacker determines your car's position.
- You try to steer to avoid other vehicles, but the hacker disables your steering and steers the car remotely, using your vehicle's cameras as a reference.
- Moments before your doom, the hacker rolls up the windows in your car, blasts the heat, and puts the radio on the highest volume setting.
- Using the car's cameras, the CIA hacker steers you off the road at the precise spot where the barrier is the only thing preventing you from dropping 500 feet.
- You crash through the barrier and go sailing off the cliff to your death, while the CIA hacker composes a text, supposedly sent from you, claiming you are tired of living and in the process of ending your life. This is sent through the car's voice to text system by the hacker.

Think this is fiction? The primary purpose of the CIA's ability to hack into cars was to perform *covert assassinations*. This isn't our term – it's theirs – straight from the Wikileaks trove of documents. A truly frightening possibility, to say the least....

How About Your Computer?

Clearly, your internet connected computer is subject to malware attacks and not just by the CIA; one can obtain malware and viruses simply by surfing the internet. The CIA goes to extra lengths to create malware for Windows because it knows full well that Microsoft Windows is the dominant operating system used by perhaps a billion or more users. The fact that the CIA can hack your computer is something most Americans suspected and believed; what was not suspected was what Wikileaks further revealed about CIA delivery methods:

- CIA has been implanting USB thumb drives and CD ROMs with malware in an attempt to reach those computers not connected to the internet.
- CIA has perfected the art of hiding data and malware within images, so that the act of opening a simple picture file can transmit malware.

Again, it's important to realize that if the CIA wants to obtain data from your computer covertly, they have literally dozens of methods at their disposal, malware being just one of them. However, in many cases, CIA malware is the *easiest* method they have, and they have become experts at disguising their software such that it is virtually unnoticeable. CIA malware on your computer is nothing at all like a virus; it does not make

21

your computer buggy or slow it down, it does not provide you, the user, with any indication that anything is wrong whatsoever. That's what makes it such an effective tool!

Just Run a Virus Check!

Many computer users rely on AVG, Symantec, MacAfee, Norton Antivirus and other similar software to guard against malware and viruses. Guess what? CIA hackers *have beaten every single one of them.* Part of the data revealed in the Wikileaks trove was extensive documentation showing that the CIA had cleverly defeated, bypassed, or rendered useless conventional antivirus software. They are just that good, and your antivirus program doesn't stand a chance against a dedicated CIA malware attack.

What Can Be Done??

At this point you're thinking, what can be done against such a powerful, formidable enemy that has unlimited funding and some of the brightest minds available on the planet? What can you, Joe American do to prevent the CIA or any other government agency from hacking you, invading your privacy, or even killing you?

Know this – the CIA is not infallible, and there are many, many ways at beating them at their own game, and not all of them involve living in a log cabin in the middle of nowhere without electricity. The CIA can, and regularly does get trumped by adversaries that are smarter than it, and CIA hackers fail to remember the old adage that if all you have is a hammer, then everything looks like a nail. Even the best CIA hacker armed with the latest malware can be beat. Let's look at some options and methods.

Rule #1: Assume every word you utter is being recorded.

Between cell phones that act as bugs to TVs with fake off modes, you are likely being eavesdropped upon and don't even know it. Be very careful of what you say with electronic devices of any kind present in the room. Consider that many homes have small rooms where no electronic devices are present (closets, mud rooms, bathrooms). Consider using these rooms to speak sensitive things in a very, very low whisper to your spouse, relative, or child. Direct communications like this in closed rooms where no eavesdropping equipment is present are *extremely* hard to listen in on, even with the CIA's powerful tools.

Rule#2: No internet = no data relay

The simple act of recording audio, video, or pictures of you is useless without the ability to transmit this data back to the CIA. The CIA uses two methods of data transmission; cell phone wireless networks for your phone, and wired or Wi-Fi internet. Absent these two transmission methods, there is no way for this stolen data to make its way back to people who can use it.

Really paranoid? *Unplug your Wi-Fi router or hub at night or whenever it's not in use.* It might be inconvenient to start it up whenever you want to use the internet (kind of like an old dial up connection), but at least data will not be transmitted without your knowledge. Also, be mindful of neighbors with Wi-Fi enabled; even if you shut your router down, the CIA can still use other Wi-Fi connections that are present...

Rule #3: Electronic devices need power to run

Sounds obvious, but an easy way to defeat a CIA hack like "fake off mode" on a TV is to simply unplug the device when it's not in use. Fake off works because the TV still has power to it by being plugged into the wall, but even the mighty CIA has not figured out how to remotely and wirelessly power devices. Worried that a device might be eavesdropping on you? Unplug it! It cannot work without power and will be unable to transmit, record, or function unless it's plugged into a wall.

Rule #4: Radio communications can be jammed

Many cell phones lack removable batteries anymore. Once upon a time, if you wanted to make sure your phone was shut off, you would just pull its battery pack (see Rule 3 above), ensuring it was dead. With a built in battery pack that isn't user removable, that's no longer an option, and if the CIA can perfect Fake Off modes with TVs, it can do the same with cell phones. So forget about trying to make sure your phone is off; take a detour and kill the phone's cell signal by putting the cell phone inside of an RF proof plastic bag. These bags are designed to keep sensitive electronics safe from static discharge, but they also have the unintended side effect of jamming the cell signal. In a pinch, you can also wrap the phone in tin foil, which does the exact same thing. With its cell signal jammed, the phone will not be able to transmit or reach the cellular network, which also means it will be useless as an eavesdropping device if it cannot transmit data back to the CIA (see Rule 2)

Rule #5: Be careful about what you commit to paper

Many terror plots are revealed before, during, or after the action because of the detailed notes that the terrorist kept; things like plans, blueprints, photos, post-it notes, hand writing on memo pads, text messages and emails all are capable of being incriminating evidence. We're not saying you are planning a terror plot, but what we are saying is that the less you write down (physically or electronically), the less the CIA will be able to use against you. The CIA cannot (as of yet) read minds, and therefore the most truly important information needs to be committed to *memory*, and if necessary, shared with trusted individuals *verbally*, in a secure location free from the threat of any eavesdropping. Memories, thoughts, and near silent verbal communication are still un-hackable by the CIA!

Rule #6: Embrace technology, but don't trust it

While new cars are exciting, fresh, and offer tons of safety features and automation, consider that perhaps you just don't need to live like the

Jetsons. Sure, a new car is nice, but a 10 year old car can be just as nice and would be totally free from the threat of remote CIA control and eavesdropping. Many of the technologies that the CIA uses to piggyback its nefarious malware on to just didn't exist even just a few years ago. Consider your safety when choosing that newer vehicle, keeping in mind that just because it has more advanced safety features than an older vehicle, doesn't mean it's necessarily *safer* for you.

Rule #7: Cell phone; friend or foe?

The cell phone is the CIA's dream device; they could not have foreseen how pervasive its use would have been in today's society. It can track your location, listen in to your calls, and read your texts and emails. It can transmit your full browsing history to anyone with a few keystrokes; it can reveal the extent of your research or ordinary life by sending your pictures to total strangers. Kids have cell phones. Grandpa in the senior's home has a cell phone. Everyone in between has a cell phone. By proximity, even if someone can't hack your phone, the phone on the table of the guy next to you can be hacked and listen in just as effectively. Cell phones are quite literally the perfect surveillance device, and at the same time, a necessity in today's society. Here's what you can do to minimize the effects of your cell:

- Don't necessarily take it with you everywhere you go. It generates a trail of where it's been, so if you need to go somewhere sensitive (cache location for example), *leave it at home*.

- Be careful what you say, write, text, browse, or photograph with the phone. Assume it's all being monitored.
- When not needed, power it down and put it in an RF proof bag.
- Run as few apps and programs on the phone as possible. Any app could be a potential vehicle for CIA malware. Go lean!

Conclusion

The CIA is a formidable adversary, but they are not infallible. It's filled with people who need to sleep, have lives and families, and have their own troubles. Although Wikileaks has exposed perhaps a sliver of their true capability, they can still be beat with common sense and some basic operational security practices. Reread the above rules and commit them to memory!